Fishing Journal

t Time: End Time:

Weather

er Temp: Air Temp:

e: Moon Phase:

L/M	S/M	Time	Weight	Length	Lure Type Color/Weight

es:_____

Time: End Time:

Weather

Temp: Air Temp:

Moon Phase:

/M	S/M	Time	Weight	Length	Lure Type/Color/Weight/N

s:_____

Start Time: **End Time:**

Weather

Water Temp: **Air Temp:**

Moon Phase:

L/M	S/M	Time	Weight	Length	Lure Type Color/Weight/

Notes:

Time: End Time:

Weather

Temp: Air Temp:

Moon Phase:

/M	S/M	Time	Weight	Length	Lure Type/Color/Weight/N

s: _____

t Time: End Time:

Weather

er Temp: Air Temp:

e: Moon Phase:

L/M	S/M	Time	Weight	Length	Lure Type Color/Weight/

es:_____

Time: End Time:

Weather

Temp: Air Temp:

Moon Phase:

/M	S/M	Time	Weight	Length	Lure Type/Color/Weight/Na

s:_____

t Time: End Time:

Weather

er Temp: Air Temp:

e: Moon Phase:

L/M	S/M	Time	Weight	Length	Lure Type Color/Weight

es:_____

Time: End Time:

Weather

r Temp: Air Temp:

Moon Phase:

/M	S/M	Time	Weight	Length	Lure Type/Color/Weight/N

s:_____

End Time:

Weather

Water Temp: Air Temp:

                               Moon Phase:

L/M	S/M	Time	Weight	Length	Lure Type Color/Weight/

Notes:_____

Time: End Time:

Weather

Temp: Air Temp:

Moon Phase:

/M	S/M	Time	Weight	Length	Lure Type/Color/Weight/Na

s: _____

Time: End Time:

Weather

Water Temp: Air Temp:

Moon Phase:

L/M	S/M	Time	Weight	Length	Lure Type Color/Weight

Notes:_____

Time: End Time:

Weather

Temp: Air Temp:

Moon Phase:

/M	S/M	Time	Weight	Length	Lure Type/Color/Weight/Na

s:_____

End Time:

Weather

Air Temp:

Moon Phase:

L/M	S/M	Time	Weight	Length	Lure Type Color/Weight

es:_____

Time: End Time:

Weather

Temp: Air Temp:

Moon Phase:

/M	S/M	Time	Weight	Length	Lure Type/Color/Weight/N.

S: _____

End Time:

Weather

Water Temp: Air Temp:

Moon Phase:

L/M	S/M	Time	Weight	Length	Lure Type Color/Weight/

Notes:_____

Time: End Time:

Weather

Temp: Air Temp:

Moon Phase:

/M	S/M	Time	Weight	Length	Lure Type/Color/Weight/Na

s: _____

Time: End Time:

Weather

Temp: Air Temp:

Moon Phase:

L/M	S/M	Time	Weight	Length	Lure Type Color/Weight

es:_____

Time: End Time:

Weather

Temp: Air Temp:

Moon Phase:

/M	S/M	Time	Weight	Length	Lure Type/Color/Weight/Na

s:_____

End Time:

Weather

Water Temp: Air Temp:

Moon Phase:

L/M	S/M	Time	Weight	Length	Lure Type Color/Weight

Notes:_____

Time: End Time:

Weather

Temp: Air Temp:

Moon Phase:

/M	S/M	Time	Weight	Length	Lure Type/Color/Weight/N.

S:_____

Weather

er Temp: **Air Temp:**

Moon Phase:

L/M	S/M	Time	Weight	Length	Lure Type Color/Weight/

es:_____

Time: End Time:

Weather

Temp: Air Temp:

Moon Phase:

/M	S/M	Time	Weight	Length	Lure Type/Color/Weight/N.

s:_____

Time: End Time:

Weather

er Temp: Air Temp:

e: Moon Phase:

L/M	S/M	Time	Weight	Length	Lure Type Color/Weight

es: _____

Time: End Time:

Weather

Water Temp: Air Temp:

Moon Phase:

/M	S/M	Time	Weight	Length	Lure Type/Color/Weight/Na

s:_____

Weather

Water Temp: Air Temp:

Moon Phase:

L/M	S/M	Time	Weight	Length	Lure Type Color/Weight

Notes:_____

Time: End Time:

Weather

r Temp: Air Temp:

Moon Phase:

/M	S/M	Time	Weight	Length	Lure Type/Color/Weight/N

s:_____

t Time: End Time:

Weather

er Temp: Air Temp:

Moon Phase:

L/M	S/M	Time	Weight	Length	Lure Type Color/Weight/

es:_____

Time: End Time:

Weather

Temp: Air Temp:

Moon Phase:

/M	S/M	Time	Weight	Length	Lure Type/Color/Weight/N

s:_____

Weather

er Temp: Air Temp:

e: Moon Phase:

L/M	S/M	Time	Weight	Length	Lure Type Color/Weight/

es:_____

Time: End Time:

Weather

Temp: Air Temp:

Moon Phase:

/M	S/M	Time	Weight	Length	Lure Type/ Color/Weight/Na

s:_____

End Time:

Weather

er Temp: **Air Temp:**

Moon Phase:

L/M	S/M	Time	Weight	Length	Lure Type Color/Weight

es: _____

Time: nd Time:

Weather

Temp: Air Temp:

Moon Phase:

/M	S/M	Time	Weight	Length	Lure Type/Color/Weight/N

s:_____

End Time:

Weather

Temp: Air Temp:

Moon Phase:

L/M	S/M	Time	Weight	Length	Lure Type Color/Weight/

es:_____

Time: End Time:

Weather

Temp: Air Temp:

Moon Phase:

/M	S/M	Time	Weight	Length	Lure Type/ Color/Weight/N.

s:_____

t Time: End Time:

Weather

er Temp: Air Temp:

e: Moon Phase:

L/M	S/M	Time	Weight	Length	Lure Type Color/Weight/

es:_____

Time: End Time:

Weather

Temp: Air Temp:

Moon Phase:

/M	S/M	Time	Weight	Length	Lure Type/Color/Weight/Na

s:_____

End Time:

Weather

Water Temp: Air Temp:

Moon Phase:

L/M	S/M	Time	Weight	Length	Lure Type Color/Weight

Notes:_____

Time: End Time:

Weather

r Temp: Air Temp:

Moon Phase:

/M	S/M	Time	Weight	Length	Lure Type/Color/Weight/N

s:_____

End Time:

Weather

er Temp: **Air Temp:**

Moon Phase:

L/M	S/M	Time	Weight	Length	Lure Type Color/Weight/

es: _____

Time: End Time:

Weather

Temp: Air Temp:

Moon Phase:

/M	S/M	Time	Weight	Length	Lure Type/ Color/Weight/N.

s: _____

Time: End Time:

Weather

Water Temp: Air Temp:

                         Moon Phase:

L/M	S/M	Time	Weight	Length	Lure Type Color/Weight/

Notes:_____

Time: End Time:

Weather

Temp: Air Temp:

Moon Phase:

/M	S/M	Time	Weight	Length	Lure Type/Color/Weight/Na

s:_____

t Time: End Time:

Weather

er Temp: Air Temp:

e: Moon Phase:

L/M	S/M	Time	Weight	Length	Lure Type Color/Weight

es:

Time: End Time:

Weather

r Temp: Air Temp:

Moon Phase:

/M	S/M	Time	Weight	Length	Lure Type/ Color/Weight/N

s:_____

End Time:

Weather

er Temp: Air Temp:

Moon Phase:

L/M	S/M	Time	Weight	Length	Lure Type Color/Weight/

s: _____

Time: End Time:

Weather

Temp: Air Temp:

Moon Phase:

/M	S/M	Time	Weight	Length	Lure Type/Color/Weight/N...

s:_____

End Time:

Weather

Water Temp: **Air Temp:**

Moon Phase:

L/M	S/M	Time	Weight	Length	Lure Type Color/Weight

Notes:_____

Time: End Time:

Weather

Temp: Air Temp:

Moon Phase:

/M	S/M	Time	Weight	Length	Lure Type/Color/Weight/Na

s: _____

End Time:

Weather

Water Temp: Air Temp:

Moon Phase:

L/M	S/M	Time	Weight	Length	Lure Type Color/Weight

Notes:_____

Time: End Time:

Weather

Temp: Air Temp:

Moon Phase:

/M	S/M	Time	Weight	Length	Lure Type/Color/Weight/N

s:_____

End Time:

Weather

er Temp: **Air Temp:**

Moon Phase:

L/M	S/M	Time	Weight	Length	Lure Type Color/Weight/

s:_____

Time: End Time:

Weather

Air Temp:

Moon Phase:

/M	S/M	Time	Weight	Length	Lure Type/ Color/Weight/N

s:_____

t Time: End Time:

Weather

er Temp: Air Temp:

:   Moon Phase:

L/M	S/M	Time	Weight	Length	Lure Type Color/Weight/

es:_____

Time: End Time:

Weather

Temp: Air Temp:

Moon Phase:

/M	S/M	Time	Weight	Length	Lure Type/Color/Weight/Na

s: _____

End Time:

Weather

...er Temp: Air Temp:

e: Moon Phase:

L/M	S/M	Time	Weight	Length	Lure Type Color/Weight

es:____

Time: End Time:

Weather

Temp: Air Temp:

Moon Phase:

/M	S/M	Time	Weight	Length	Lure Type/Color/Weight/N

s:_____

t Time: End Time:

Weather

er Temp: Air Temp:

: Moon Phase:

L/M	S/M	Time	Weight	Length	Lure Type Color/Weight/

es:_____

Time: End Time:

Weather

Temp: Air Temp:

Moon Phase:

/M	S/M	Time	Weight	Length	Lure Type/Color/Weight/N

s:_____

End Time:

Weather

Temp: **Air Temp:**

Moon Phase:

L/M	S/M	Time	Weight	Length	Lure Type Color/Weight

es:_____

Time: End Time:

Weather

Temp: Air Temp:

Moon Phase:

/M	S/M	Time	Weight	Length	Lure Type/Color/Weight/Na

s: _____

End Time:

Weather

er Temp: **Air Temp:**

Moon Phase:

L/M	S/M	Time	Weight	Length	Lure Type Color/Weight

es:_____

Time: End Time:

Weather

Temp: Air Temp:

Moon Phase:

/M	S/M	Time	Weight	Length	Lure Type/Color/Weight/N

s: _____

Time: End Time:

Weather

...er Temp: Air Temp:

:   Moon Phase:

L/M	S/M	Time	Weight	Length	Lure Type Color/Weight/

...es:_____

Time: End Time:

Weather

Temp: Air Temp:

Moon Phase:

/M	S/M	Time	Weight	Length	Lure Type/Color/Weight/N

s:_____

End Time:

Weather

Water Temp: **Air Temp:**

Moon Phase:

L/M	S/M	Time	Weight	Length	Lure Type Color/Weight

Notes:_____

Time: End Time:

Weather

Temp: Air Temp:

Moon Phase:

/M	S/M	Time	Weight	Length	Lure Type/Color/Weight/Na

s:_____

End Time:

Weather

Temp: Air Temp:

Moon Phase:

L/M	S/M	Time	Weight	Length	Lure Type Color/Weight

es:_____

Time: End Time:

Weather

Air Temp: Air Temp:

Moon Phase:

/M	S/M	Time	Weight	Length	Lure Type/Color/Weight/N

s:_____

End Time:

Weather

Water Temp: Air Temp:

Moon Phase:

L/M	S/M	Time	Weight	Length	Lure Type Color/Weight/

Notes:_____

Time: End Time:

Weather

Temp: Air Temp:

Moon Phase:

/M	S/M	Time	Weight	Length	Lure Type/Color/Weight/N：

s:_____

t Time: End Time:

Weather

er Temp: Air Temp:

e: Moon Phase:

L/M	S/M	Time	Weight	Length	Lure Type Color/Weight/

es:_____

Time: End Time:

Weather

Temp: Air Temp:

Moon Phase:

/M	S/M	Time	Weight	Length	Lure Type/Color/Weight/Na

s: _____

t Time: End Time:

Weather

er Temp: Air Temp:

e: Moon Phase:

L/M	S/M	Time	Weight	Length	Lure Type Color/Weight

es:_____

Time: End Time:

Weather

Temp: Air Temp:

Moon Phase:

/M	S/M	Time	Weight	Length	Lure Type/ Color/Weight/N.

s:_____

Weather

Water Temp: Air Temp:

Moon Phase:

L/M	S/M	Time	Weight	Length	Lure Type Color/Weight/

Notes:_____

Time: End Time:

Weather

Temp: Air Temp:

Moon Phase:

/M	S/M	Time	Weight	Length	Lure Type/Color/Weight/N

S:_____

t Time: End Time:

Weather

er Temp: Air Temp:

e: Moon Phase:

L/M	S/M	Time	Weight	Length	Lure Type Color/Weight

es:___

Time: End Time:

Weather

Temp: Air Temp:

Moon Phase:

/M	S/M	Time	Weight	Length	Lure Type/Color/Weight/Na

s:_____

Start Time: _____ **End Time:** _____

Weather

☀️ ⛅ 🌬️ 🌧️ ⛈️

Water Temp: _____ **Air Temp:** _____

Date: _____ **Moon Phase:** _____

L/M	S/M	Time	Weight	Length	Lure Type Color/Weight

Notes: _____

Time: End Time:

Weather

r Temp: Air Temp:

Moon Phase:

/M	S/M	Time	Weight	Length	Lure Type/Color/Weight/N

s:___

t Time: End Time:

Weather

er Temp: Air Temp:

Moon Phase:

L/M	S/M	Time	Weight	Length	Lure Type Color/Weight/

es:_____

Time: End Time:

Weather

Temp: Air Temp:

Moon Phase:

/M	S/M	Time	Weight	Length	Lure Type/Color/Weight/N

s: _____

t Time: End Time:

Weather

er Temp: Air Temp:

e: Moon Phase:

L/M	S/M	Time	Weight	Length	Lure Type Color/Weight/

es:_____

Time: End Time:

Weather

Temp: Air Temp:

Moon Phase:

/M	S/M	Time	Weight	Length	Lure Type/ Color/Weight/Na

s:_____

t Time: End Time:

Weather

er Temp: Air Temp:

e: Moon Phase:

L/M	S/M	Time	Weight	Length	Lure Type Color/Weight

es:_____

Time: End Time:

Weather

Temp: Air Temp:

Moon Phase:

/M	S/M	Time	Weight	Length	Lure Type/Color/Weight/N

s:_____

End Time:

Weather

Temp: Air Temp:

Moon Phase:

L/M	S/M	Time	Weight	Length	Lure Type Color/Weight/

es:_____

Time: End Time:

Weather

Temp: Air Temp:

Moon Phase:

/M	S/M	Time	Weight	Length	Lure Type/Color/Weight/N.

s: _____

End Time:

Weather

Water Temp: Air Temp:

Moon Phase:

L/M	S/M	Time	Weight	Length	Lure Type Color/Weight

Notes:_____

Time: End Time:

Weather

Temp: Air Temp:

Moon Phase:

/M	S/M	Time	Weight	Length	Lure Type/ Color/Weight/Na

s:_____

Start Time: _____ End Time: _____

Weather

Water Temp: _____ Air Temp: _____

Date: _____ Moon Phase: _____

L/M	S/M	Time	Weight	Length	Lure Type Color/Weight

Notes:_____

Time: End Time:

Weather

r Temp: Air Temp:

Moon Phase:

L/M	S/M	Time	Weight	Length	Lure Type/Color/Weight/N

s: _____

Weather

er Temp: Air Temp:

Moon Phase:

L/M	S/M	Time	Weight	Length	Lure Type Color/Weight/

es:___

Time: End Time:

Weather

Temp: Air Temp:

Moon Phase:

/M	S/M	Time	Weight	Length	Lure Type/Color/Weight/N.

s:_____

End Time:

Weather

Temp: Air Temp:

Moon Phase:

L/M	S/M	Time	Weight	Length	Lure Type Color/Weight

es:___

Time: End Time:

Weather

Temp: Air Temp:

Moon Phase:

/M	S/M	Time	Weight	Length	Lure Type/ Color/Weight/Na

s:_____

t Time: End Time:

Weather

er Temp: Air Temp:

e: Moon Phase:

L/M	S/M	Time	Weight	Length	Lure Type Color/Weight

es:____

Time: End Time:

Weather

Temp: Air Temp:

Moon Phase:

/M	S/M	Time	Weight	Length	Lure Type/Color/Weight/N

s:_____

End Time:

Weather

Temp: Air Temp:

Moon Phase:

L/M	S/M	Time	Weight	Length	Lure Type Color/Weight/

es:_____

Time: End Time:

Weather

Temp: Air Temp:

Moon Phase:

/M	S/M	Time	Weight	Length	Lure Type/Color/Weight/N...

S: _____

End Time:

Weather

Water Temp: Air Temp:

Moon Phase:

L/M	S/M	Time	Weight	Length	Lure Type Color/Weight

Notes:_____

Time: End Time:

Weather

Temp: Air Temp:

Moon Phase:

/M	S/M	Time	Weight	Length	Lure Type/Color/Weight/Na

s:_____

End Time:

Weather

Water Temp:　　　　　Air Temp:

　　　　　　　　　Moon Phase:

L/M	S/M	Time	Weight	Length	Lure Type Color/Weight

Notes:_____

Time:			End Time:			
			Weather			

Temp: Air Temp:

Moon Phase:

/M	S/M	Time	Weight	Length	Lure Type/Color/Weight/N	

s:_____

t Time: End Time:

Weather

er Temp: Air Temp:

Moon Phase:

L/M	S/M	Time	Weight	Length	Lure Type Color/Weight/

es:_____

Time: End Time:

Weather

Temp: Air Temp:

Moon Phase:

/M	S/M	Time	Weight	Length	Lure Type/Color/Weight/N.

s:_____

t Time: End Time:

Weather

er Temp: Air Temp:

:   Moon Phase:

L/M	S/M	Time	Weight	Length	Lure Type Color/Weight/

es:_____

Time: End Time:

Weather

Temp: Air Temp:

Moon Phase:

/M	S/M	Time	Weight	Length	Lure Type/Color/Weight/Na

s:_____

End Time:

Weather

Water Temp: Air Temp:

Moon Phase:

L/M	S/M	Time	Weight	Length	Lure Type Color/Weight

Notes:_____

www.ingramcontent.com/pod-product-compliance
Lightning Source LLC
LaVergne TN
LVHW020422080526
838202LV00055B/4999